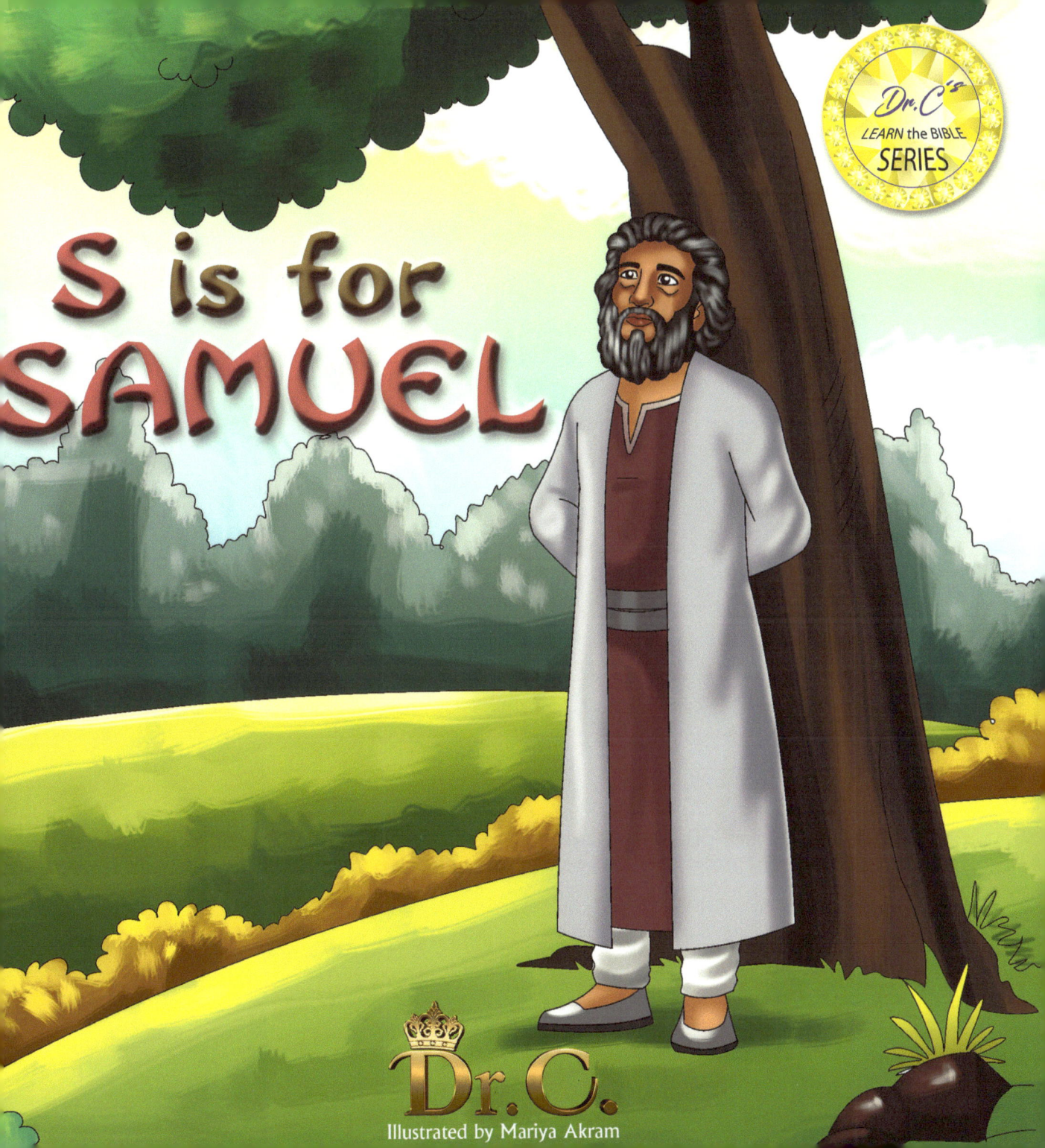

www.clfpublishing.org
909.315.3161

Copyright © 2022 by Cassundra White-Elliott.

All rights reserved. No portion of this book may be reproduced, stored in a retrieval system, or transmitted by any form or any means electronically, photocopied, recorded, or any other except for brief quotations in printed reviews, without the prior permission of the publisher.

Cover design by Senir Design. Contact info: info@senirdesign.com

Illustrations by Mariya Akram of Fivver.com

ISBN #978-1-945102-79-0

Printed in the United States of America.

Dedicated to

Zuri Dior White (Precious)

and

Kimara Tsehai Faith White (Little Lady)

Once upon a time, long long ago, in a land far far away, a baby was born. The baby was a gift from God, and his birth was a miracle. The baby's name was Samuel, and he was born to Hannah, a woman who had wanted a child for a very long time but was unable to have one. Finally, God answered her prayer and gave her a son. Hannah promised God she would give her child back to Him for His service.

After Hannah had stopped breastfeeding Samuel, she took him to Eli, the high priest, who would train and guide him in his service to God.

As Samuel learned from Eli, he ministered before the Lord, while wearing a special robe. The robe was made by his mother, who would make him a new one each year and take it to him.

When Samuel was much older, he heard a voice calling him while he lay sleeping. He thought the voice was coming from Eli. So, he went to Eli's room to see what he wanted. When Samuel reached Eli's bedside, Eli said he had not called out to Samuel. Samuel went back to his room. Later, Samuel heard his name two more times. Each time he heard the voice, he went to Eli, but it was not Eli who was calling him. Eventually, the two realized Samuel was hearing the voice of God.

From that point, Samuel grew in wisdom and became God's prophet. Then, with the wisdom he had, he began to serve as one of Israel's judges, judging the different situations the people were involved in. Day in and day out, people would approach Samuel with their questions and problems. Samuel would give the people the answers God gave him.

Then, as time went on, the people of God began to desire an earthly king to rule over them and to watch out for their best interests, even though God had been doing that all along. They believed Samuel was too old to lead and guide them. And even though God had always met the needs of the Israelites, they wanted an earthly king like the pagan nations they were surrounded by. Hearing their requests, God decided to give the people a king.

God chose a man named Saul to be the first king of the Israelites. However, before the king could serve the people, he had to be anointed. God chose Samuel to anoint Saul by pouring olive oil on his head. From that point, Saul served as king, and for a while he was a very good king.

Along the way though, Saul began to make some bad choices, and God was not happy. Saul did not follow God's instructions. Instead, he did what he wanted to do. Samuel told Saul, "Obedience is better than sacrifice," (I Samuel 15:22). God decided Saul would not remain as the king of the Israelites. He wanted someone who would follow instructions and do what was best for the people.

Finally, God decided it was time for a new king. So, God sent Samuel to Bethlehem to anoint the person who would serve as the second king of Israel. That person was David, who was only seventeen years old at the time he was first anointed. By the time David was 33, he was seated upon the throne to serve as king.

Samuel lived a long and full life as God's servant, from the time he was a toddler to the time he was an old man. He was always faithful to God, following God's instructions. And, God was well pleased with Samuel's life.

www.ingramcontent.com/pod-product-compliance
Lightning Source LLC
Chambersburg PA
CBHW041933160426
42813CB00103B/2913